An introduction

Wellbeing is at the very heart of how we function well as human beings and by taking a proactive approach to life, we can enhance it.

So, what is wellbeing?

Wellbeing is about our overall quality of life and is ultimately determined by our social, economic and environmental conditions.

It is also worth bearing in mind that wellbeing is a much broader concept than being just about our mental and physical health. There are many other aspects that we need to consider and we can benefit from embracing a more holistic approach to help balance our lives better. By taking some time to reflect on each aspect of our life and where we can make improvements, we will be able to cope well with change and life's inevitable challenges.

Having spent many years researching a variety of life skills to support our wellbeing, my aim with this book is to distil some of that information and share a collection of practical tips that I have learnt along the way.

I do hope that you enjoy this book and most of all that it provides you with a few nuggets of wisdom.

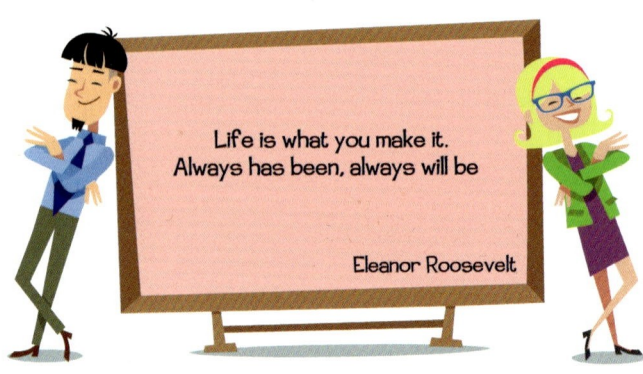

Be proactive about your wellbeing

One of the greatest lessons that I have learnt in life and especially around building personal resilience is how important it is to be proactive about our overall wellbeing. Raising self-awareness and creating time and space for personal reflection can help us to understand what areas we need to focus on and improve. We are all unique and one size doesn't fit all, so my advice with this book is to treat it like a thought buffet of ideas and suggestions and take away what works best for you.

By giving ourselves the opportunity to consider what we are doing well in our lives and what areas we can improve on we can then build our own personalised wellbeing toolkit. Taking personal responsibility for our wellbeing is essential and this will help us to be more resourceful, resilient and fit for the future.

The Seven Wisdoms of Wellbeing

Wellbeing is so much more than looking after our mental and physical health and this model outlines seven significant areas that we all need to embrace so that we can take a more comprehensive approach.

Emotional wellbeing – How we can constructively channel our emotions to maintain positive mental health
Physical wellbeing – How we can combine healthy eating, exercise, relaxation and sleep to manage our energy, stress levels and support our immune system
Social wellbeing – How we can build great relationships and support our community
Financial wellbeing – How we can make well informed choices to enjoy life, both now and in retirement
Digital wellbeing – How we can manage the influences and impacts of technologies and digital services
Environmental wellbeing – How we can occupy and support a healthy, enjoyable and stimulating environment
Spiritual wellbeing – How we can find meaning and purpose in our lives

Action tip – It is helpful to set aside some time to review all these aspects of wellbeing and score yourself out of ten for each. You can then begin to explore which of these areas you need to pay attention to and work on.

Throughout this book we will take a deeper dive into some of these areas, and I will also share my top three tips for each one.

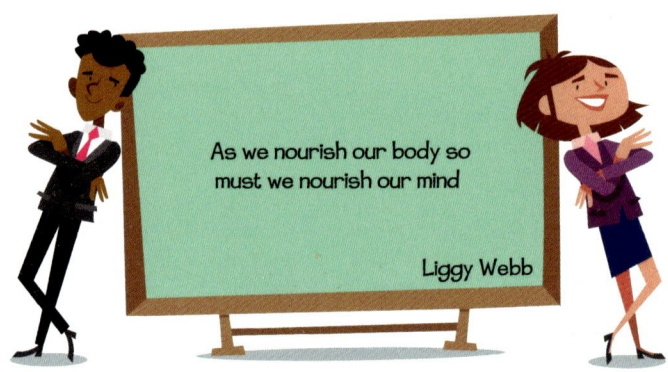

1. Emotional wellbeing

Emotional wellbeing is an aspect of our mental health and is essentially about our ability to cope with both positive and negative emotions and this also involves our awareness of them. When we understand how to constructively channel our emotions, we will be able to positively support our mental health.

Our internal mind-chatter can have a big impact on how we feel because our brain digests whatever thoughts we create, so learning how to reframe some of our internal dialogue can be helpful. I often think of words as nutrients for the mind and the quality of the thoughts that we feed ourselves with will provide the best fuel for our mind. Learning to reframe some of the negative vocabulary we may use into something more positive and constructive can have a big impact on how we feel.

Here are some more of my favourite tips to support emotional wellbeing.

Tip one – Improve your stress intelligence

I truly believe that the most important relationship that any of us can have in our life is our relationship with stress. Stress is part of the human condition, and we will all experience elevated stress levels and stressful periods. If we become overwhelmed and even push ourselves to the point of burnout it will have a damaging impact on our emotional wellbeing.

My advice is to work on your stress intelligence. This can be done by raising self-awareness of what our stress triggers are, understanding how our stress manifests itself both emotionally and physically, and being aware of what healthy (and unhealthy) coping mechanisms we may use to deal with increased stress levels.

Tip two – Take a daily dose of gratitude

Taking a daily dose of vitamin G (vitamin gratitude) can be such a wonderful tonic. Setting aside some time each day, to think about things that we are grateful for, can be so beneficial for our emotional wellbeing. When we get into a negative spiral taking time to focus on what we are grateful for can be uplifting and life-affirming. An attitude of gratitude can work wonders for our mood.

A great deal of research around positive psychology has identified that gratitude is strongly and consistently associated with happiness and resilience. Taking time daily to focus on things we are grateful for can help us to experience more positive emotions, improve our overall health, deal better with life's challenges and build stronger relationships.

Keeping a daily gratitude journal, using a tactile object such as a gratitude stone and sharing our daily highlights with others are all a great place to start.

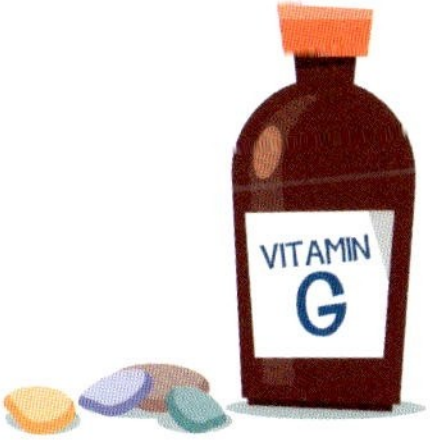

Tip three – Reach out for support

First of all, I would like to emphasise that reaching out and asking for support is a sign of courage not weakness. We are all human and with that comes a whole host of vulnerabilities and fragilities. One of the reasons I am committed to the work that I do around wellbeing has much my own personal experience with depression. It can be a very dark place and it is absolutely nothing to feel ashamed about as so many people experience mental health problems at some point in their lives.

Being able to talk to someone about how we feel can be so cathartic and it is also the first step to getting any other necessary support we may need. It is also very comforting to know that we are not alone and on this journey that we call life, we are all in it together.

2. Physical wellbeing

Our physical wellbeing is a combination of healthy eating, exercise, relaxation and sleep so that we can manage our energy and stress levels and support a healthy immune system. Looking after our physical wellbeing can reduce our chances of disease and infection and help us to enjoy our lives in a more fulfilling way.

We are creatures of habit and getting into good habits can be a challenge. Most of us know what we need to do, however, keeping on track isn't always easy. There are, however, a few fundamental things that we do that will have a positive impact.

Here are my top three tips for improving physical wellbeing.

Tip one – Get moving

Regular physical activity is one of the most important things we can do for our health and whatever our capacity it is important to be as active as we can. This will help to improve our brain health, manage our weight, reduce the risk of disease, strengthen bones and muscles, and improve our ability to do everyday activities.

Getting outside for some fresh air every day can be so invigorating and especially in the winter months. I would also recommend yoga and Pilates. One of my favourite mantras is "motion is the lotion" and this reminds me to do some stretching as often as possible, especially if I have been sitting at my desk for a long time. So, within your capacity, do your very best to "get moving".

Tip two – Have a rest

One of my favourite quotes is by the Roman poet Ovid who once said, "Take a rest, a field that has rested gives a bountiful crop." This is such wisdom. We need to rest to be able to replenish our energy levels and recharge. So often in this fast-paced and busy world that we can forget how important it is to do that. One tip is to put some rest time in your diary or on your to-do list each day and view resting as a priority and an opportunity to refuel. The better we pace ourselves, the more productive we will be.

It is also worth bearing in mind that without good quality sleep we won't function as well. Good quality sleep is as essential to our bodies as eating, drinking and breathing because sleeping helps to repair and restore our brains as well as our bodies. We spend approximately a third of our lives asleep and getting into good sleep habits will have such a positive impact on both our emotional and physical wellbeing.

Tip three – Fuel yourself well

We are essentially what we consume and fuelling ourselves well is fundamental for our overall wellbeing. We are made up of water, protein, fat, minerals and vitamins and every single molecule comes from the food we eat and the water we drink. Making sure we avoid junk food and embracing a nutritious and balanced diet will help us to achieve our highest potential for health, and vitality.

Keeping hydrated is also very important and one of the most valuable things that we can do to stay healthy and energised. Drinking water is vital for all our bodily functions and not only does water flush out toxins, it is the building block for almost every single fluid our bodies make.

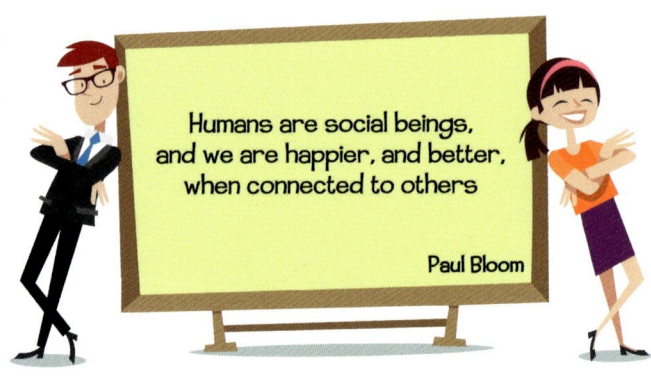

3. Social wellbeing

Social wellbeing is about building and maintaining healthy relationships in our lives and having meaningful interactions with those around us. It provides us with a sense of belonging and involves communication, boundary setting, and mutual respect regardless of our differences. Cultivating and maintaining an optimal level of social wellbeing can have a big impact on our self-esteem and sense of belonging.

Engaging well with other people in our homes, workplaces and communities will also help us to understand how we can make a positive contribution. Keeping regular contact with our friends and family, spending quality time with our loved ones, engaging well with work colleagues and volunteering are all helpful ways to boost our social wellbeing.

Here are a few more tips.

Tip one – Empathise with others

One of my favourite phrases when it comes to describing empathy is "your heart in my heart" and our desire to want to put ourselves in someone else's shoes and understand how they may be feeling is one of the most powerful gifts we can give to anyone. By being empathetic we can help other people feel less lonely and more supported.

Humans are social beings, and we all have the capacity to develop empathy which enables us to build stronger and more supportive relationships. Like any other behavioural skill, empathy can be cultivated through intentional effort and practice. By being empathetic we can better "read" another person's inner state and interpret it without being judgmental, giving advice or attempting to fix the situation.

Tip two – Listen well

Listening and empathy do, of course, go hand in hand, and listening is one of the most powerful and constructive ways that we can demonstrate empathy. When we practise active listening, we are listening with purpose and with a deep desire to want to really hear what someone is saying. This helps us to understand people better, which ultimately helps us to forge stronger and more meaningful relationships.

Everyone you meet knows something that you don't and being curious about other people and deeply listening to what they have to say can be a fascinating experience. In this hyper-distracted world we may also need to remind ourselves to be fully present when we are with someone and this will help us to be a much better listener.

Tip three – Be a great collaborator

Our daily lives are fuelled by collaboration and as individuals we are entwined with others in so many areas of our lives. Many of the decisions we make will affect other people in some way or another. Being a great collaborator can have a big impact on our social wellbeing and is about cooperation and coordination and relies on our willingness to want to listen, understand and learn from each other.

To collaborate well we need to be able to communicate effectively with each other and be prepared to pull together and cooperate as part of a team effort. Successful collaboration can be hugely rewarding and success tends to taste a lot sweeter when it is shared with others.

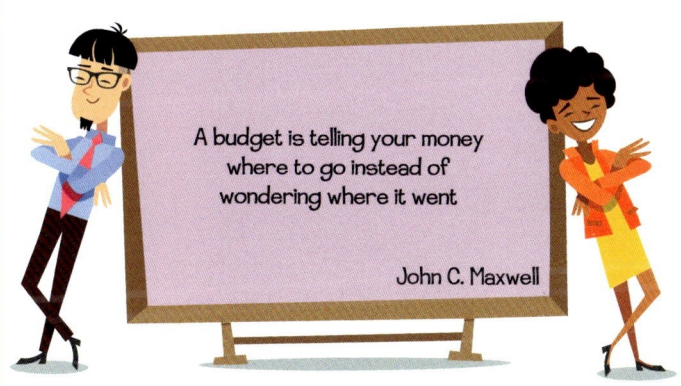

4. Financial wellbeing

Many financial experts that I speak to describe financial wellbeing as feeling secure and in control of our finances, both for now and for the future. It is about knowing that we can pay our bills, deal with the unexpected, and are on track for a healthy financial future right through to retirement and beyond.

In times of economic challenges, it is becoming increasingly important to get the best advice and support as possible. Financial safety brings security and peace of mind and can have a big impact on our overall wellbeing.

I have spent time with various financial advisors and have curated the following top three tips.

Tip one – Educate yourself

One sure way to boost our financial wellbeing is to improve our financial literacy and this is about our ability to understand and apply different financial skills effectively, including personal financial management, budgeting and saving. This, ultimately, will help us to be more self-sufficient, so that we can maintain better financial stability and confidence.

There is a lot of good advice out there and it is well worth setting aside time to explore what support is available. Many organisations offer financial wellbeing support as part of their employee assistance programmes. If we are worrying about our finances, it is important that we reach out and get some advice and support because ignoring any financial problems will only lead to more anxiety and stress in the future.

25

Tip two – Budget

Out of all the advice that I have received about financial wellbeing right at the top of the list has been how important it is to plan our spending and budget. This helps us to take control and decide where we need and want to spend our money. This will, of course, include essentials like our rent or mortgage payments, utility bills and transport and then more of the non-essential items.

Planning our spending and budgeting helps us to gain more confidence over our finances because we can see exactly what we are spending our money on and how we can make savings where necessary. Setting aside time to forecast our spending each month is a great habit to get into and there are lots of apps that can be helpful and save you time too.

Tip three – Be resourceful

Financial resourcefulness involves being well-organised, knowing our financial goals, and finding effective ways to reach those goals. Seeking advice from a financial professional is a good place to start as they can help us to understand how we can make our money work best for us.

It is also helpful to look at ways to be less wasteful and more resourceful. There are so many little things that we can do to save money. In a disposable society where we may hanker after the next new shiny thing, sometimes we have to ask ourselves if it is really necessary. So next time you go to throw something away and replace it, take a good look and see whether it's repairable or reusable. If we do this, not only will we be helping our bank balance, we will also be protecting our planet.

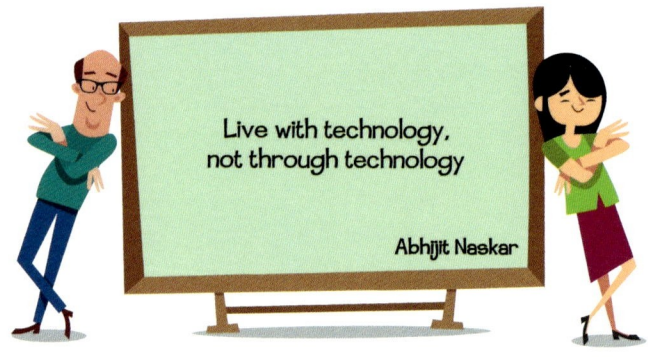

5. Digital wellbeing

Digital wellbeing is about how we positively manage the influences and impacts of technologies and digital services. By raising awareness of some of the challenges of living and working with technology, we can build our capability and establish healthy boundaries.

Technology plays a big part in most of our lives these days and, ideally, technology and the internet should be there to enhance and simplify and have a positive impact on our lives. This isn't always the case and how we choose to interact with technology is fundamental to our overall wellbeing.

Here are three of my favourite tips to boost our digital wellbeing.

Tip one – Embrace the future

We are currently living with a great deal of technological advancement and it is anticipated that there will be emerging breakthroughs in a whole host of different areas that will include artificial intelligence, robotics, autonomous vehicles, biotechnology, nanotechnology, quantum computing and the Internet of Things. What lies before us is mind-boggling! In the next phase of industrialisation, it is predicted that humans will work alongside advanced technologies and AI-powered robots to enhance processes within the workplace.

Positively embracing the future, being open-minded and seeking out opportunities to upskill our technological capability will help us to feel more confident about any technology as it evolves.

Tip two – Manage mobile technology

I came across a term recently known as "phubbing", which apparently is about "snubbing" people in favour of our phones when a text/call comes through or sitting scrolling through social media when in company. I am sure we have all experienced this. It is definitely worth being aware of how we interact with social media and our mobile phones when we are in the company of others as it can impact on our relationships and social wellbeing.

We also need to be mindful of how we engage with social media. Whilst it can be a great way to share information and bring people together it has its pitfalls too. Multiple studies have found a strong link between heavy social media use and an increased risk of depression, anxiety, loneliness and even self-harm. Like everything in life, we need to establish helpful boundaries and find a healthy balance.

Tip three – Switch off

Unplugging from technology and taking a technoholiday offers multiple benefits. It can reduce stress and anxiety, improve our sleep, boost our physical wellbeing and ultimately help our productivity. Creating moments of sanctuary and being able to switch off from time to time throughout the day can help us to rest and recharge. If we are constantly switched on it will drain our batteries and have a detrimental impact on our wellbeing.

Technology can be addictive so if your first impulse when you get a quiet moment is to reach for your device, remind yourself of some of the other more meaningful and relaxing things that you can do. Choose instead to go outside and get some fresh air and go for a lovely walk around nature. Listening to some music or even just taking a few moments to do some deep breathing can help us to switch off and feel more relaxed.

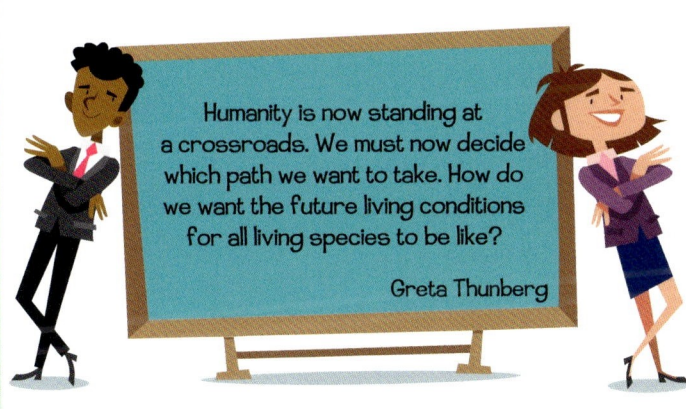

6. Environmental wellbeing

Environmental wellbeing is about occupying and supporting a healthy, enjoyable and stimulating environment. There are many ways that we can boost our wellbeing in this way. This may be about raising awareness of our personal space and how we can create an environment that is more conducive to our overall wellbeing. It can also be about appreciating the natural world around us and making the most of the health benefits of being around nature.

Environmental wellbeing is also about the role we play as far as climate change is concerned. It is about what we can do, in our everyday lives, to minimise damage and help make the planet more sustainable for the future.

Tip one – Simplify and declutter

Do you ever feel stressed and overwhelmed when you look around and see lots of mess and clutter in your home, study place or work environment?

Overloading ourselves and carrying too much unnecessary baggage will slow us down and can even be a cause of anxiety. There is a great deal to be said for simplifying our lives and decluttering. The art of keeping things simple and tidy can reduce stress and give us more time and space for the things we value.

Getting rid of what we don't use, need or love can be so liberating and energising. It is easier to prepare healthy meals in a clutter-free kitchen and we will sleep much better in a tidy bedroom. Decluttering can also reduce dust, mould and mildew, which may trigger asthma and allergies. By simplifying and decluttering we can also save money by learning to be more resourceful and less wasteful.

Tip two – Appreciate the natural world

Being around nature is the foundation of our health, wellbeing and prosperity and exposure to the natural world is beneficial for all of us as human beings. Connecting with nature can boost our mental health and contribute to our physical wellbeing by reducing blood pressure, regulating heart rate, easing muscle tension and managing stress levels.

There are so many ways that we can bring nature into our everyday lives, from indoor or outdoor gardening, exercising in the fresh air, relaxing by water, exploring green spaces and being around insects and animals. Any way that we can connect with nature will have a positive impact and, whatever the weather, it is so beneficial to get outside every day.

Tip three – Make a positive impact

We can all play a part in limiting climate change. From the way we travel, to the electricity we use and the food we eat, we can all make a positive impact. What are you doing to make a positive impact?

If you would like a free copy of this digital poster, please email liggy@liggywebb.com

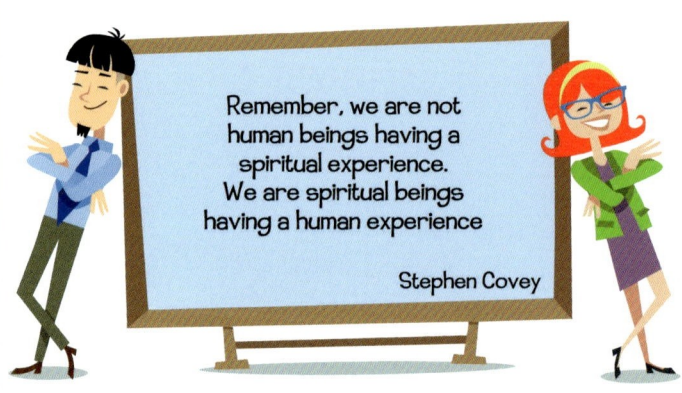

7. Spiritual wellbeing

Spiritual wellbeing relates to having meaning and purpose in our lives and is essential in supporting our overall wellbeing. This can involve our connection to our community, culture, spirituality and religion and includes the beliefs, values and ethics we hold dear to us.

Spiritual wellbeing can help us to feel more motivated and enhance the quality of our lives. It can also help us to deal well with challenging situations and manage anxiety, stress and depression by helping us to cultivate inner peace and hope.

Here are my top three tips on how we can bring more meaning and purpose into our lives.

Tip one – Discover your ikigai

One interesting way to explore our purpose and meaning is through "ikigai" which is a Japanese concept and a word that translates into "a reason for being". Ikigai is the union point of four fundamental components of life: passion, vocation, profession and mission. It helps guide people towards taking actions which can improve the quality of our life experience and promotes a sense of meaning and purpose.

It's worth taking the time to ponder these questions. Am I good at what I do? Do I love what I do? Does the world need what I do? If you can say yes to all those questions, then you have discovered and achieved your ikigai.

Tip two – Explore your faith

Whatever your faith, places of worship can provide a great environment for us to connect with others and build a strong sense of community and support. Finding someone or an organisation that shares our values and beliefs will help us to bond with like-minded people who can support and encourage us.

If we don't have a particular faith community then another way to help us feel connected to our spirituality and faith is to explore a cause that matters to us so we can make a positive contribution. We may decide to volunteer for a charity we are passionate about, become a mentor or tutor or even foster an animal. Doing any of these things can help us to support our community and will provide us with a sense of purpose and meaning because we will be contributing to what we believe in and what matters to us.

Tip three – Be kind

Being kind is an important way of bringing meaning to our own life as well as bringing joy and happiness to the lives of those around us. It is a way that we can spread goodness in the world and make a positive difference.

In many ways, kindness can be contagious because when we see someone do something kind or thoughtful, it can inspire us to be kinder. In this way, kindness spreads from one person to the next, influencing the behaviour of people who perhaps didn't even witness the original act in the first place. Kindness is the glue that connects people and it is the key to supporting a healthier, happier and psychologically safer world. No act of kindness is ever too small.

So, what next?

I do hope that you have enjoyed this book and that it has helped you take a more holistic view of wellbeing. My advice is to take some time to reflect on the wellbeing wheel below and review the scores that you may have given yourself in the exercise at the beginning of the book. Take some valuable time to think about where you need to focus your attention and what improvements can be made.

It is also well worth exploring what may be available for you as many organisations and workplaces now provide some excellent resources and employee assistance programmes, so it is worth seeing what is available.

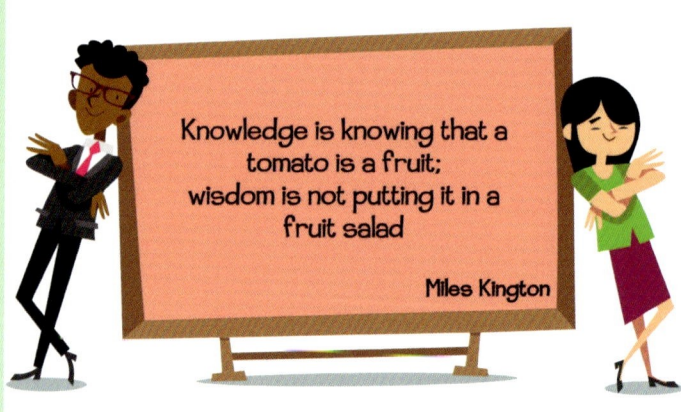

Take action

When it comes to wellbeing, the real wisdom is what we do with all the information and knowledge we acquire along the way. Please do remember it isn't always about what we know, it's what we do with that knowledge that will make the difference to our overall wellbeing. So, on that basis, action is required!

Whatever it is that we intend to do we will be far more likely to achieve it if we set out a clear action plan. I have created a free electronic version of this action plan to help achieve goals and if you would like a free copy then please do email liggy@liggywebb.com

Be curious and keep learning

We are all people in progress and we never stop growing and our personal potential is limitless. Embracing lifelong learning and the power of curiosity will help us to thrive and adapt well in a constantly changing world. Learning can boost our wellbeing and this may explain why our brains are evolved to release dopamine and other feel-good chemicals when we encounter new things.

If you would like more tips and advice on a range of different topics to support wellbeing, then please visit my website and blog www.liggywebb.com/blog

Also, do join me on Linkedin where I host a microblog called "The Wisdom of Wellbeing".

Life is better when we keep learning.